REMEMBERING JESUS

The Poiema Poetry Series

Poems are windows into worlds; windows into beauty, goodness, and truth; windows into understandings that won't twist themselves into tidy dogmatic statements; windows into experiences. We can do more than merely peer into such windows; with a little effort we can fling open the casements, and leap over the sills into the heart of these worlds. We are also led into familiar places of hurt, confusion, and disappointment, but we arrive in the poet's company. Poetry is a partnership between poet and reader, seeking together to gain something of value—to get at something important.

Ephesians 2:10 says, "We are God's workmanship . . ." *poiema* in Greek—the thing that has been made, the masterpiece, the poem. The Poiema Poetry Series presents the work of gifted poets who take Christian faith seriously, and demonstrate in whose image we have been made through their creativity and craftsmanship.

These poets are recent participants in the ancient tradition of David, Asaph, Isaiah, and John the Revelator. The thread can be followed through the centuries—through the diverse poetic visions of Dante, Bernard of Clairvaux, Donne, Herbert, Milton, Hopkins, Eliot, R. S. Thomas, and Denise Levertov—down to the poet whose work is in your hand. With the selection of this volume you are entering this enduring tradition, and as a reader contributing to it.

—D.S. Martin
Series Editor

COLLECTIONS IN THIS SERIES INCLUDE:

Six Sundays toward a Seventh by Sydney Lea
Epitaphs for the Journey by Paul Mariani
Within This Tree of Bones by Robert Siegel
Particular Scandals by Julie L. Moore
Gold by Barbara Crooker
A Word In My Mouth by Robert Cording
Say This Prayer into the Past by Paul Willis
Scape by Luci Shaw
Conspiracy of Light by D. S. Martin

Remembering Jesus

Sonnets and Songs

JOHN LEAX

CASCADE *Books* • Eugene, Oregon

REMEMBERING JESUS
Sonnets and Songs

The Poiema Poetry Series

Cascade Books
An Imprint of Wipf and Stock Publishers
199 W. 8th Ave., Suite 3
Eugene, OR 97401

www.wipfandstock.com

ISBN 13: 978-1-62564-560-9

Cataloging-in-Publication data:

Leax, John

Remembering Jesus : poem / John Leax.

The Poiema Poetry Series 11

viii + 52 p. ; 23 cm.

ISBN 13 : 978-1-62564-560-9

1. American Poetry—21st century. I. Title. II. Series.

PS3562.E262 2014

Manufactured in the USA.

To

My friends

In the Chrysostom Society

Past and present

The

Peace of Christ

Table of Contents

Prayer

Matthew 26:25, 27:5

I dream of grace. The tongue that might have praised,
That might have sung forgiveness equal to
The sum of all the mercy God shot through
Creation when his stone-sealed Son blazed
Awake, the light to light betrayal's dark
Design, is swollen black in the hole that was
A mouth; my brother, Judas, hanged the ark
Of his redemption. Still I dream of grace.
I dream I take him from his tree, and lift
Him up to life. Should one betrayal cost
A soul—eternity demand such thrift
Of grace—the lost remain forever lost?

How then my three denials be forgiven?
Christ, Savior, win your chosen back for Eden.

Zacharias

Luke 1:5–41

Elizabeth became my voice when all
My praise was silence, doubtful words by angel
Presence stopped in mercy, my faith too small
For careless acquiescence to the marvel
He announced. In silence I became a sign
Of grace Elizabeth conceived. Her touch
Brought me alive to wordless bliss, divine
Intention whole in broken love such
As we know in cruel diminished age.
Joy swollen, she hid herself. God's silence
Binding me, I lived, a walking suffrage,
Before the coming incandescence.

When Mary came, our Joy leapt up included
To greet the one in virgin womb secluded.

Old Shepherd

Luke 2:13–14

As winter cold leans hard upon my back,
I long for once-upon-a-time when I
Was small enough my elders watched the black
Night through and let me sleep. Only the cry
Of the ewe in lambing time caused them to make
Me rise; my hands were small to ease a birth.
I minded them and rose. This night I shake
Beside the fire. Wind blowing from the north,
Disturbs the boy I used to be. No stars
Blanket his sleep. Once to voices brilliant
In light I woke. We found a child not far
From where we kept our sheep. Rough celebrants,
We woke his mother from her careful rest.
Like a lamb newborn he nestled at her breast.

In Rama There Was a Voice

Matthew 2:16–18

"The king requires your son," I said. No more
Herself than a child, the infant's mother turned
Her head. Her hand closed white against the door.
She knew an end had come. Her silence earned
Her mercy I refused. I took the life
She held and stepped outside. How does one kill
Before a mother's eye? Not with sword or knife.
Not with thrusts that once begun would fill
A street with blood. I cradled the infant
And mouthed into its ear a lullaby.
Over its puckered mouth I closed a tyrant's
Frightened hand. I squeezed so it could not cry.

The mother-child clutched my arm. The night
Became a winding sheet. There was no light.

Resurrection Song: With Money in their Hands

Matthew 29: 11–15

What you must say you won't find hard
The elders told the hapless guards:
Say He was stolen while we slept.
His thieves will spin the world, except
We make a truth of our canard.

No judge will find your sluggard
Hour fair cause to launch hard
Words at you or to suspect
What you must say.

The guards obeyed the elders' word
And told of bodies, haggard
And overcome when starless night crept
Round the stone-locked crypt.
With money in their hands it was not hard
To say what they would say.

Recognition

John 2: 14–15
Luke 2: 48

There was, I thought, something about the man
Familiar, an image pressed on the coin
Of memory. But slow, afraid I'd join
The fallen under toppled tables, I ran.
I'm sure, now, I needn't have. His harsh whip
Sought the rash of thieving profiteers
Hawking oxen, sheep, and pigeons, their sneers
Mocking country pilgrims come to worship.

I crept back when breath returned. Around
Him stood the Pharisees. His zealousness
For the Father's house brought back a scene. Years
Ago I watched a quiet boy confound
The elders. As then, I saw his brightness
Was a sword. His mother's love would end in tears.

Zebedee

Matthew 4:21–22

Two sons I gave the Lord. Not willingly.
Our shadows stretched across the narrow shelf
To where the deep water darkens Galilee.
The night of labor ended, I knew myself
As blessed. Two faithful sons, a crew of hands
To pull a weight of fish that I alone
Would lose. Such easy work to give commands!
Such joy to see them jump. The light that shone
Upon my back was good. A net profit
Rose each morning. Laughter filled each day.
Then Jesus, working the rocky shore, thought
To call, "James, John." They left my net, my way,
And followed. Risen, he calls me, "Zebedee,"
And keeps me mending nets beside the sea.

The Sixth Man

John 6:34

I was a taking sort of man and she
A woman, worn by giving, satisfied
To trade a mockery of love. Her fee—
Nothing elaborate, a place beside
Another, a protective touch, a hand
Restrained when annoyance flares. I took her in.
Asking little of her, I was more bland
Than eager in my need. A simple bargain
Bound us until the prophet at the well
Requested water, spoke her holy name,
And told her story true. She ran to tell
Us all. Her rescued heart leaped aflame.
Like a desert bush, it burned. Afraid of fire,
But drawn, I fell before her great desire.

The Centurion's Servant

Matthew 8: 5–13

I lay awake. The household noise about
Me called. I did not answer. Locked within
My paralyzed body, my voice cried out.
Alone, I felt my broken words begin.
They ended at my lips. I raised my hand;
It stayed beside me on the bed. I knew
Suddenly, among men, I'd become an island.
I watched bereft as they withdrew.
How long I lay distressed I cannot say.
My mother, Sorrow, held me to her breast,
And then, as if it were her gift to weigh
The cost of birth, she smiled. I was blessed:

The one I served had found the One we serve.
Grace, from afar, chose a house to conserve.

A Good Joke

Mark 2: 5

My bitter carping drove four friends to haul
My stiffened carcass up onto the roof.
They'd had their limit of my spewing gall,
My endless invective, complaints—God's proof
I stank of sin. They tore the tiles away,
Dislodged debris on crowding crowds below.
They laughed as I sputtered, clinging halfway
Off the mat they handed down. "Don't let go,"
I cried. Their eager faces ringed the ceiling
When Jesus looked up. "Your sins are forgiven,"
He said to me. That was not the healing
I desired. Scowling, I saw them shaken
By gleeful laughter. My end is comedy!
I laughed in truth and laughter made me free.

Sower

Mark 4: 1–3

The grapes are dark. The wheat is golden. Soon
The harvest I sowed in spring will bend my spine.
My years, like the mounting sun of afternoon,
Bear down, too great a weight to ease with wine.
Still, yet a little while, I'll bend to keep
My hillside strung with vines, my level field
In grain. This daily joy of work and sleep,
Of offered care shall be my heart's strong shield
Against the waste of awful time. I heard
A rabbi tell a parable of seed cast
On every soil. He toyed with the absurd.
What wakes in me that moment so long past?
The lake? That distant boat, holy in sunshine?
This work: wheat into bread, grapes into wine?

Resurrection Song: The Glad Earth Quaked

Matthew 28: 2–4

Beside the stone at the garden wall
The guards kept easy watch. The small
Hours passed. The almond air beguiled
Their senses through the nights while
Christ lay bound in swaddling pall.

There was no darkness to appall,
Just darkness fragrant to enthrall,
Until the sudden angel
    Tossed the stone aside.

Like dead men, fallen at the wall,
The guards lay still. Within his stall
Of stone, Christ rose, the docile
Son now clothed in King's apparel.
The glad earth quaked; the angel
    Tossed the stone aside.

A Certain Man

Luke 8: 26–39

However long delayed his coming, Christ
Knew the country of my mind. In me dark
Spoke to dark. In him light was every word
The Father and the Spirit told the Son
Within that unity of three in one.
I ranged among the stony tombs. Monarch
Of death, a voice in me called, "Christ, I've heard
Your name. Shall I tell you mine? I'm Legion."
In naked savagery, many, not one,
We raged. Then suddenly, bright emptiness!
A filling unimaginable, flame
On flame of searing grace, and words to bless
That Name, holy above every name.
Once many, I've come to rest, One, in Christ.

Given Our Disposition

Matthew 8: 28–34

Good Greeks, we aspire to order. Acts
Like his joke plummeting healthy pigs down
A cliff risk chaos. Our demoniacs
Disturb the tombs; they never rouse the town.
At most they spook the poor inhabiting
The storm scoured caves in the rough terrain
Above the springs where bathers ease small pains
In calming, bubbling heat. Prohibiting
Another violation of our rule
Seemed wise. Prophets needn't come in power,
Wielding it to make a city cower.
Gadera has room for chain-breaking ghouls,
for noisy demons wise enough to fear his name.
Jerusalem killed him. Our city bears no blame.

Daughter

Luke 8: 49–56

I don't remember. I was twelve, not yet
Aware of how a parent dies before
A child's bewilderment. I lay beset
By fever, lost to life. I will not bore
You reconstructing how they called my name
And wept. They were, perhaps, more deeply stricken
Than some, my father's leadership a claim
On God's beneficence. I've forgotten—
I don't remember anger. No. What stays
With me is waking to voices about
My bed, one voice clear in the haze
Of wonder, and my father's joyous shout.

So long ago now! I live bound by that surprise
And long to hear again that voice, "Daughter, arise."

Simon Muses

Matthew 10: 1–5

My son, be still awhile; old men, zealous
In youth, grow tired. The spirit stays; the flesh
Departs—slowly, slowly—each day a fresh
Betrayal. Laughter, however, grows joyous.
The comedy is whole. Christ's outrageous
Grace, betrayed, redraws the traitor's brash
Design. He, who swerved, was my friend, that rash
One who launched the Savior's perilous
Passage out of time into the present
Of this green island where my death awaits.
So many miles, so many souls ago,
The accountant and the joker were sent
To learn humility. Then we walked straight,
Paired, yoked, like oxen to turn the furrow.

There is no authoritative history of the life of Simon. One of the many legends told of him places him in England at the time of his death.

Fisherman's Dream

John 6: 1–21

A boy, eager for excitement, I chased
The crowd along the shore. Disaster surely
Awaited—shipwreck, bodies, bones, the waste
Of life. But not that. A man, lovely
Of voice netted me with stories. I stayed.
The sea was still and quiet. The sun spoke
On the hillside. We lingered. The voice played
The hours short. Then sudden hunger broke
The calm.
                    I love this hour of shadows flung
Shoreward by light behind my boat. I heed
Once more the work-rough hand on my arm, the one
Who took my fish and took my bread to feed
The host. Some nights I sail out on the lake
And dream he follows walking in the wake.

Spy

John 6:15

There was much grass where we found him. Rain fell
Freely on the slopes, feeding the swift Jordan.
Below us we could see the lake, its swell
Bright in sunlight. I saw him turn to scan
The rising wave of our approach. Sorrow,
Like a cloud, passed over him. He made us sit.
He knew our hunger's nature. The meadow
Rippled at his word. Grass and flesh, Spirit
Fed, rose up. But only the grass's praise was true.
He slipped away. I saw and followed up
The mountainside. At last in solitude
He crushed beneath his knees the wild hyssop.

Ashamed I turned away, and turned a stone.
He heard. My spying heart was overthrown.

Resurrection Song: Terror Seized the Three

Mark 16:8

Terror and amazement seized the three,
When entering the dark where he
Was laid. Sitting on the tomb's right,
A young man dressed in white
Announced, "Jesus is gone to Galilee."

They did not speak the trembling three.
In grief they fled. Their hearts unsteady,
Arrhythmic in the shining light
Of terror and amazement.

Christ on his chosen tree
Cried, "E'loi E'loi la-ma sabach-tha'ni."
They knew his body broken, tight
Bound by sin's cruel might.
What could they do but flee
In terror and amazement.

Bethzatha

John 5:2–9

An angel troubled the pool—so legend said.
Helplessness made us believers. Six years,
Waiting in the portico, I leaned my head
Against the wall, never a volunteer
To lift my twisted body down the stairs.
No matter; no angel rippled the long pool
With healing waves. So many huddled there,
Bound in sheep gate stench—the fetid wool
of sacrifices bought and sold for sins
the wealthy owned. Once a roaming rabbi
spoke, "Stand up!" to a crumpled bag of skin
beside me. It stood. I clawed the stone. My dry
voice called to the rabbi's back. He did not turn.
Forsaken, empty, I've nothing more to learn.

Three Ends

Mark 6: 14–29

1. Salome
Mark 6:22

I danced. Oh how I danced. My body made
The music flesh. My hands having become
The motion of the circling spheres, the sum
Of men's desire, I slipped through the palisade
Of Herod's wit unveiled. I could have stayed
His blind extravagance; I chose gruesome
Satisfaction, mother's anger. Welcome
At his side I might have had, gold and jade.

I never danced again to please his court.
Nor, once she had her death, did my mother
Choose to let me near. She loathed my face.
I grieve my beauty given to extort
John's head. Ancient now, and gross, I cover,
My fat with silk, a gown of squandered grace.

2. Herod Antipas

Mark 6:26

Intrigue made him king of the Jews. Blood made
Him hated. His end: an inflammation
Of the lower bowel, mortification
Of the testes. The cry of innocents betrayed
The helplessness of power I would learn
In fear. Forced upright by the agitation
Of his breath, he brought down jubilations
Of death on those who after him would govern.

From his will I received my crown. A worm
With aspirations, my revolution—
A stolen bride, a slain prophet, a lost war—
Bought me this exile, this Gaul, this long term
In a bitter bed. I long for restitution.
God, bring my prophet back! Restore! Restore!

Herod the Great ordered the slaughter of the innocents. His son Heron Antipas beheaded John the Baptist and conspired with Pontius Pilate in the crucifixion of Jesus. The emperor Caligula banished Antipas to Gaul in 37 CE. Herodias accompanied him in his exile.

3. Herodias

Mark 6:24

A stratagem. Never was I without
A stratagem. Philip and Antipas
Learned my cleverness too late to shout
Me down or twist my willfulness to loss.
Both fell before my whims. Philip I threw
Aside. The simple wealth his bed bestowed
Was short of what I craved. Antipas drew
Me. Power, hardened in his heart, echoed
Our sounding dreams. Then that wild man,
That locust-crunching lout awoke my rage.
Miscalculation's end is exile. Roman
Justice lines my face deeper than age.
Embittered Antipas tastes of vengeance;
His tongue darts deadly as my child's dark dance.

Leper

Luke 17:16

The ten of us stuck together—decay
our common bond, foul ulcerated skin
Our distinction. Jew and Samaritan
We scavenged beside the border highway.
It was a bleak existence. Day after day,
Our fingers clawed tighter. To know again
The wholeness of our lives before this ruin,
We cried to halt the teacher's journey.

He sent us to the temple priest. Along
The way, my hands opening, my flesh now bright
And infant soft, my heart beat with gratitude.
I would, I thought, be His. But I thought wrong.
I loved too much my wife. Her touch at night
Stole from my heart my chosen servitude.

Samaritan Leper

Luke 17:16

Remember me? I was once an eager friend,
A raucous youth, not shy at love or drink.
But then the brownish spots that would not mend,
The nodules swelling, bursting. The horrid stink!
My gift for touch stolen, my life truncated
With my fingers, I grieved every gesture
Of affection from afar. Each grated
On my skin. My daily loss was torture.
My voice, least among the exiled ten, cried,
"Master, Jesus." He told us, "Go. Show
Yourselves to the priests." Twice defiled, satisfied
No priest would free me of my sorrow,
I returned to him. His service is my end.
I return to you, by grace, a better friend.

Resurrection Song: And They Remembered His Words

Luke 24:1–8

Inside the tomb the women found
Their emptiness—no body wound
In grief's relentless, mournful prose.
From solid rock confusion rose;
It multiplied their pain. No sound

Escaped that hollowed ground.
Then shining in the stone-lined round
Two angels stilled their sorrows,
          Inside the tomb.

Heaven's High Spirit found
Comedy in the underground.
Like the lightning gleam of their clothes,
The electric word the angels chose
Became the grace in which they drowned
          Inside the tomb.

The Young Ruler

Mark 10:20–22

Laughter followed when I turned away.
I'd run to him; he required all I had.
"A rich man," he said, as I moved off, "is a
Camel at the needle's eye." Was he mad?

I love the law. With David I can say
It's hidden in my heart. Then laughter broke
My scowl and rose in me. No halfway
Measure, deep throaty yielding to the joke.

Days later, I returned. My camels sold
To profit others, shyness overcame
My want to catch his eye. The parable
He told contained and eased my shame.

Two sons were called. One balked. One gave ascent.
He lied. The first one tamed his will and went.

At Ephraim with the Disciples

John 11:54

1. When Joseph Died

They talked sometimes at night, when crickets rasped
Their legs in song. They thought I slept. They thought
They kept the remembered terror tightly grasped
In whispers, but I heard. A king had sought
My life and theirs. We came to rest from years
Of exile, but Nazareth was never home.
My laughter underwrote the silent tears
That lined their hearts like water scoring stone.

When Joseph died, I asked, at last, to know
What they had hidden. Mother shook her head
As if she knew some greater pain would grow
With knowledge. Her voice was heavy with dread.

Burdened, my hands seek the touch of wood,
The comfort of work, the memory of good.

2. With His Eyes

When Joseph died, the wood he'd stacked to dry
Was handed down to me. I'd learned from his hand
The skill to sight along the beam and try
The grain for true. I remember how I'd stand
By his side watching the saw ripping the wood
Lengthwise, the dust rising gold in sunlight.
It was as if his work by God's grace could
Center the neighborhood in blessing. My sight
Stayed fixed on him until he turned, one day,
Placed in my hands a rule and made me see
With his eyes. His teaching made straight my way.
I thought that he was all that I should be.

I was happy at his work, though he was gone.
Then the Word came to my cousin John.

3. The Work of Wood

The shavings curled from my plane the afternoon
She stood, a shadow in the door, and spoke
The single syllable. I thought, *So soon.*
But deep in me a harmony awoke,
A rhythm lost in the hammer song I made
Furnishing the world, chair by chair, bed by bed.
Her single word was *Go*. My debt was paid.
Joseph's memory would be satisfied:
My craft would find its end in speech—the Word
Voiced as once when spoken it divided light
From dark and all Creation bloomed. I heard
My father in her voice. Both sadness and delight
Indwelt the shop, as if the two were one
As they may be when the work of wood is done.

Nazarene

Mark 6:2

No one disliked Mary. We knew her past
Included rumors, a journey into
Egypt for private, suspect reasons few
Heard and fewer believed. The contrast
Of their lives—Joseph's careful work and silent
Constancy, Mary's calm alignment
To his will—prevented righteous scrutiny.

Even Jesus, that doubtful son, we held
In favor until he claimed authority
To speak of holy things. Who taught him wisdom
That we should marvel? Our hearts rebelled;
Our knowledge of his base heredity
Kept us safe in Herod's brokered kingdom.

Villager

Luke 19:30–35

"The Lord has need of it," he replied and made
Me wonder if he knew the colt was mine.
I watched as he undid the braided line
That tethered it. I wasn't quite afraid,
But an authority in his voice stayed
My hand. His assurance seemed to define
Our given places in a grand design
That claimed obedience. We both obeyed
And made together an extravagance
Of trust. Without a warrant other than
That need, we joined the lineage of promise.
We did not know the reach of violence
Or that the course of willful actions ran
Through death, our mercy bought by a traitor's kiss.

Resurrection Song: On the Road

Luke 24:13–31

A stranger met their open fear,
Their disappointed hope, their clear,
Afternoon darkened by
The memory of the cross-torn cry,
And the Roman's piercing spear.

What comfort could they find so near
Jerusalem? In light austere
Their talk like dust was dry.
  Who was that stranger there?

They walked within an atmosphere
Of pain. Should death with life cohere?
They did not know. Their tongues would try
The truth beneath the azure sky,
What truth they knew lay on its bier.
  Who was that stranger there?

A Woman of the City

Luke 7:36–39

How the alabaster jar of ointment came
Into my hands is a story mothers tell
To sons they love, as if dull words could tame
The urge that rings in flesh like death's sweet knell.
Forget that. Begin with me weeping, crouched
At the teacher's feet, road-calloused, dirt-caked,
Unwashed by the preening Pharisee slouched
Satisfied at the table. My tears snaked
Down my Savior's instep. My unbound hair
Fell loosely and dried the kisses I'd
Lavished with the ointment. I was all need. The air
Swirled with perfume as if a king had died.
My touch moved him! I felt his life quicken!
One word made me his forever—*forgiven.*

Malchus

John 18:10

Few things I did, I did by choice. The way
Of Caiaphas left little room for one
Whose life was servitude. My every day
And night was his. Obedience won
Safety, never approbation. I served
To keep his temper calm. The faith I kept
Was to myself. The night the torches curved
A line through the garden to intercept
The Nazarene who'd stirred the wayward crowd
With signs, I marched in front. His burly friend
Slashed off my ear. "Jesus," I cried aloud.
His quick touch brought my bleeding to an end.

So what! Damn both priest and demon magus!
My faith stands firm; Malchus stands for Malchus.

A Palace Guard

John 19:2–3

Falernian held rank and place by wit.
He was good wine, and we were glad to drink.
A perfect fool, no clown, he knew the limit
Of indulgence. His fall-ripe instinct
Turned jokes into reward. The night the Jews
Gave up their king he scored his very best.
Passing beside a buckhorn hedge, he drew
A knife and cut a shoot. Our interest
Pricked, we watched him braid a ring to toss
Onto the fire. But quick to pleasure power,
His twist made it a crown. The double-cross
Of priest and friend joined blood and splendor.
We robed the king in purple, mocked, "Lord, Lord,"
Marched him to the skull, and pierced him with a sword.

Pilate's Wife

Matthew 27:19

Their cursed religion complicated night
And day. Samaritans contrived to make
Vitellius ignore the rumbling earthquake
Of rebellion in that land and take delight
In playing us for fools. Had we been tight
With him instead of Antipas, awake
To how the end of innocence would shake
Our throne, the world might yet be bright.

That night the Jews betrayed their king, my dreams
Were dark; I suffered many things. I warned,
"Do nothing to that man." He washed his hands,
Then crossing god, he yielded judgment. Suborned
Witnesses bought us these empty mountain lands.
I dwell distraught where waters lie in moonbeams.

Pilate's rule as procurator ended when he chose to suppress a Samaritan rebellion. The Samaritans appealed to Vitellius, legatee in Syria, who had Pilate summoned to Rome to answer charges before Tiberius. Tiberius, however, died before Pilate reached Rome, and there is no record of what happened to Pilate. One legend has both Pilate and his wife becoming Christians. Another has Pilate die a suicide by order of Caligula. A third legend has Pilate drown himself in Lake Lucerne after spending a period of exile in the mountains with his wife.

Rufus

Mark 15:21

By travel hardened, father had seen Roman
Expedience at work and kept as far
From it as Cyrenean wisdom—the chosen calm
Of one schooled in the ordered grammar
Of renunciation—allowed. His habit was
To step aside. No momentary pain
Nor pleasure defined an adequate cause
To break his discipline. He bore the strain
Of the awkward cross, then standing straight, turned
Aside at the dismissive word, "You're done."
He did not stay to see salvation earned
By Christ for soldier, thief, and sage. His son,
I've learned the folly of that turning. In Rome,
I pray with Paul: Christ Jesus, call him home.

Mother

Luke 23:42–43

Bitter my name should be. My mother's watch
Beneath the cross, my son hanging in day-
Light dark, endures. No moment in a notch
Of passing time, I walk there now. It is my way.
Hope holds me yet in that hour when I heard
My son, whose voice could bring sullen people
To the edge of insurrection, find the Word
Till now unknown. Nailed to his grim pole,
He rounded to the truth. "Jesus, when you come
Into your kingdom," he begged, "remember me."
Christ turned as still he turns when hearts plumb
True and spoke, "Today with me you will be
In Paradise." The Word addressed my son!
My grief! My grief enthrones God's Holy One.

Resurrection Song: Our Gardener Christ

John 20:11–16

One at his head, one at his feet,
Between them lay the winding sheet.
The angels neither sang nor wept,
When Magdalene who had not slept
Bent down into the tomb. Her fleet

Tears tracked her furrowed face like sleet.
What in the angels' words discreet,
Renewed the darkened hope she kept?
Our gardener Christ the risen king.

They spoke no comfort sweet,
No truth she might accept,
And yet they planted in her heart, bereft,
The seed of joy to burst, to greet
Our gardener Christ the risen king.

Lazarus

Luke 23:42–43
John 11:43–44

"This day," Jesus promised the thief, "you shall be
With me in Paradise." I've thought on that
Long hours of this my second life. I see
Little. I toss through sleepless nights. What
I remember is at odds with the Word
Suspended on the cross that moment before
He gasped and dropped into the still discord
Of sin. What change he must have worked! More
And more I worry the bone of my dismay.
Fever I recall—and Martha's soothing hand—
Mary hovering—and then the voice to obey—
"Come out:" that irresistible command.
    Four days I lay senseless on my cold stone.
    Those days were naught. The end remains unknown.

Bystander

Mark 15:34–37

I gave him sour wine which he refused.
Remembering that small particular—
The gesture, at once, strange and familiar—
Perturbs my mind. His face, turned aside, bruised,
And blood-striped, judged our justice, accused
The wanton wielding of law's hammer
To cross him off the earth. I heard him stammer
A broken sentence; I heard his Word confused.

He succumbed too quickly to satisfy
Our mocking hearts. We watched three men die
Forsaken in the darkened noonday light.
Why should that one turning from me occupy
My hours of troubled sleep? Why do I cry
"My God, my God" in the anguished night?

A Friend of Joseph

Luke 23:48–49

Too many years, my Miriam. Our end
Is hard upon us. Eyes are made to see
Loveliness in age, to see the dividend
Of work in faith confirm the blessed tree
Of fathers giving up to sons the labor
First given them by Him who loves. (His purpose
Be affirmed.) Miriam, life is vapor.
In Sheol mercy is forgetfulness.
I would go there now and soon forget. My old
Friend's son! I remember him—a youth
Dancing his load of wood across a scaffold
As lightly as a Roman judge holds truth.

Sweet Joseph safely dead. He did not see
That dancing son nailed to his bitter tree.

In a Garden of Decapolis

John 12:20

We muse on hints and guesses, truth misheard
By ears both sharp in youth and clogged in age.
We know, at best, we cannot know—a rampage
Of questions quieted by years. Absurd
This want of certitude. Once a word
From Bethsaida, faint like a scent in foliage,
Reached us. We went from village to village
Finding only stories confused and blurred,
Retold to suit each teller. Jerusalem
Brought no better end. A prophet rose and fell
Before we tested him. These things we fear:
Our time is but the cycle of the year.
Truth is this garden where seeds die and swell.
Apart from the root, there is no stem.

The High Priest's Maid

Mark 14:66–70

The courtyard fire collapsed, its light falling
Into itself, its warmth withdrawing from
The night. I laid fresh thorn on it, stalling
The creep of cold against the coming kingdom.

One stood nearby, obscured in cloaking shadows.
In the quick flare of the thorn I knew his face:
"You are with Jesus?" I asked. He swore, "God knows,
I'm not." And he was not—except by grace.

Nor then was I; the rope of lawless dread that bound
Christ's friend bound me. He fled, a mutineer,
Sinking in the night as once he nearly drowned,
His drifting eyes turned inward on his fear.

The Spirit lifted him at Pentecost:
His fiery word retrieved me from the lost.

Before Patmos

John 19:25–27

My mother, the mother of my Lord, lay still,
Blankets of years drawn close about her face.
Her quiet heart, the Spirit's domicile
Within her, measuring her life in grace,
She gave no sign. Neither joy nor sorrow
Disturbed her eyes. Wordless then, the prayer
Delivered to her swelled like an embryo.
Her silence, incarnate in the morning air,
Soft as an infant's hand, held me at her side.
Willingly I stayed. I raised her head.
I brushed her lips with water. Her calm belied
My grief. She bore the weight of love perfected .

Jesus, Savior, this also is your cross—
The fierce endurance of our mother's loss.

Resurrection Song: The Beloved Disciple

John 20:2–9

Four women braved the sorrow of the cross.
With them, broken, lingered one disciple.
He was the one on whom the sun had risen,
But there, lined by shadow, he knew the light
Devoured by dark. He knew Creation
Suffered, the end common to all of life.

He did not know of Patmos, of exiled life
Secluded in His holy cave across
The sea of persecution. There, Creation
Would confirm his solitude, disciple
Him in stark austerity. There, the risen Christ
Would permeate the shining island light.

Nor did the women know the way Christ's light
Would thrust away the stone, abundant life
Burst all confinement. To know Him risen,
They would endure with Him His death, then cross
The three-day darkness adrift on lost Creation's
Raft, accompanied by that loved disciple.

At the women's word, that swift disciple
Easter morning ran to meet the breaking light,
And as he ran, unknown to him, Creation
With its rising sun received His vernal life.
The angel at the tomb rejoiced, "He is risen!"
And death hung pinioned on its bitter cross.

Then death, despairing on its bitter cross,
Cried, "Naught has come to naught." The disciple,
Halting by the tumbled stone, felt, risen
In his heart, bright hope. He saw the angel light,
But still he did not comprehend Creation
Born anew, infused with resurrection life.

For him the taste of resurrection life
Came that dawn the fisher Christ called across
The water, "Come and eat." The new Creation
Of his heart and mind obeyed. Christ's disciple,
Born again, he ate the feast of his risen
Savior and knew the truth of morning light.

Receiving light, he made the light his life.
Islanded, at last, he rises in prayer to cross
The sea, this Creation—Christ's loved disciple.

Simon the Magus

Acts 8:22–24

I did not always live this way, alone,
Withdrawn, refusing pilgrim strangers
Inquiring of me a word to make known
The mystery troubling them like hunger.
Neighbors' children come now, bringing bread,
Asking nothing more than my smile. I give
It freely and the prayers I have said,
Without their understanding that we live
By grace. Grace came to me by Peter's curse.
Through his hands, his word, the Spirit descended.
For that power I reached out my purse;
In quiet I repent how I offended.

Here, in children's voices, in bread and wine,
The Spirit lives. Here, light as a child, I dine.

Church tradition has not been kind to Simon the Magus. The sin of purchasing church office bears his name, and Dante places Simon in the eighth circle of Hell along with a number of Popes who are punished by being suspended upside down in narrow holes with flames licking the soles of their feet. Irenaeus believed Simon to be the founder of Gnosticism, and other sources portray him as a constant opponent of Peter. It may be, however, that the Samaritan Simon of Acts has been confused with a different Simon Magus. This confusion leaves open a more generous judgment of Simon, one that takes the repentance expressed in Acts 8:24 as genuine.

Acknowledgements

Copyright © June 12, 2007 by the Christian Century. "The Work of Wood" is reprinted by permission from the June 12, 2007 issue of *The Christian Century.*

Copyright © April 21, 2009 by the Christian Century. " Daughter" is reprinted with permission from the April 21, 2009 issue of *The Christian Century.*

Copyright © May 19, 2009 by the Christian Century. "Prayer" is reprinted with permission from the May 19, 2009 issue of *The Christian Century.*

Made in the USA
Lexington, KY
02 June 2018